GUATEMALA

by Joanne Mattern

LOOK!
BOOKS™

Red Chair Press   Egremont, Massachusetts

Look! Books are produced and published by Red Chair Press:

Red Chair Press LLC   PO Box 333   South Egremont, MA 01258-0333

www.redchairpress.com

Publisher's Cataloging-In-Publication Data

Names: Mattern, Joanne, 1963-

Title: Guatemala / by Joanne Mattern.

Description: Egremont, Massachusetts : Red Chair Press, [2019] | Series: Look! books : Hello neighbor | Interest age level: 004-008. | Includes index, Now You Know fact boxes, a glossary and resources for further reading. | Summary: "Guatemala and the United States share many things and also have many differences. But like any neighbor, it is good to know how we are alike and how things are different. Readers will discover the beauty of Guatemala's land, animals, and cities while discovering how children's lives are like their own and how they differ."--Provided by publisher.

Identifiers: ISBN 9781634403856 (library hardcover) | ISBN 9781634403870 (paperback) | ISBN 9781634403863 (ebook)

Subjects: LCSH: Guatemala--Social life and customs--Juvenile literature. | Guatemala--Description and travel--Juvenile literature. | United States--Social life and customs--Juvenile literature. | United States--Description and travel--Juvenile literature. | CYAC: Guatemala--Social life and customs. | Guatemala--Description and travel. | United States--Social life and customs. | United States--Description and travel.

Classification: LCC F1463.2 .M38 2019 (print) | LCC F1463.2 (ebook) | DDC 972.81 [E]--dc23

LCCN: 2017963408

Photo credits: iStock except for the following; p. 11: J Marshall - Tribaleye Images/Alamy; p. 20: loca4motion/Alamy; p. 21: Yaacov Dagan/Alamy

Printed in the United States of America

0918 1P CGS19

Table of Contents

All About Guatemala

Hola! (OH-la) from Guatemala! *Hola* is how you say "hello" in Guatemala.

Guatemala is in Central America. It is next to Mexico. Guatemala is a small country. The Caribbean (kuh-RIB-ee-uhn) Sea is on one side of Guatemala. The Pacific Ocean is on the other side.

UNITED STATES

Gulf of Mexico

CUBA

MEXICO

Bahía de Campeche

Carribbean Sea

BELIZE

HONDURAS

GUATEMALA CITY
★

GUATEMALA

EL SALVADOR

NICARAGUA

COSTA RICA

PANA

North Pacific Ocean

5

Guatemala once belonged to Spain. In 1821, it became an **independent** country.

Guatemala's flag is blue and white. The two blue stripes stand for the two oceans on each side of Guatemala. The white stripe in the middle stands for peace and purity. Guatemala's **coat of arms** is in the middle of the flag.

Good to Know

The bird on the Guatemalan flag is the quetzal. The quetzal is the country's national bird. The eagle is the national bird of the United States.

7

The **capital** of Guatemala is Guatemala City. About one million people live there. In 1917 and 1918, earthquakes destroyed the city. The city was rebuilt after the earthquakes.

Guatemala's money is called the quetzal like the national bird.

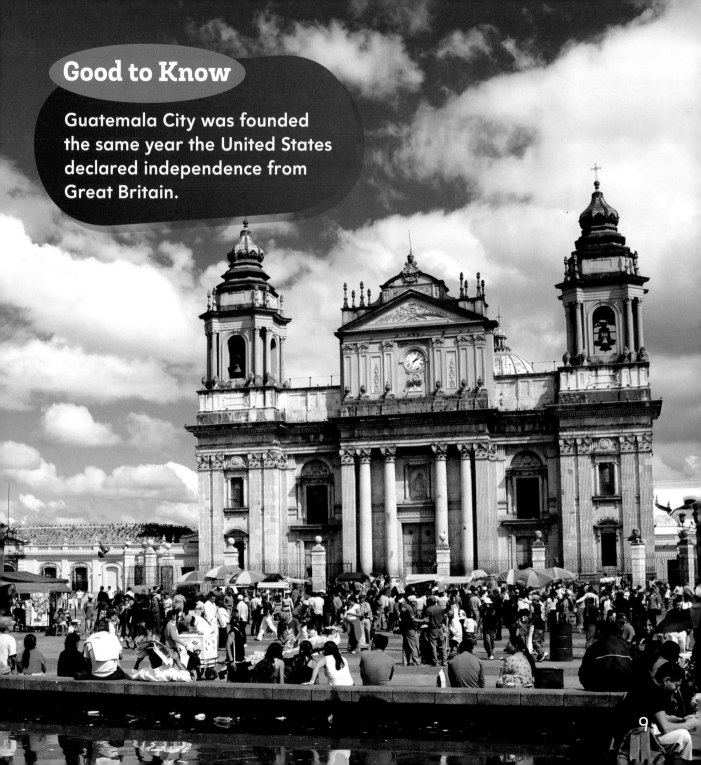

The Land

Guatemala is a land of volcanoes. There are more than 30 volcanoes in Guatemala. Three of them are active. A volcano called Tajumulco is the highest point in Guatemala. It is 13,846 feet (4,220 meters) tall.

Good to Know

There are volcanoes in the United States too. Most of them are in Hawaii and Alaska.

Most of Guatemala is made of mountains. They are called the highlands. The climate in the highlands is cool and dry. Most Guatemalans live in the highlands.

Guatemala also has lowlands. They are along the coast. The climate in the lowlands is hot and wet. Many **rain forests** are found along the rivers and lakes.

Animals

Many unusual animals live in Guatemala. One large animal is the tapir. Large cats include the jaguar, puma, and mountain lion.

tapir

Guatemala is home to 750 kinds of birds. Many birds, like hummingbirds and parrots, have bright colors. The quetzal is one of the most beautiful.

Good to Know

The jaguar is the third largest cat in the world. Only lions and tigers are bigger.

15

Guatemala's waters
are full of life!
Many different
sea turtles
lay their eggs
on the beach.
Colorful fish
and rays swim in
Guatemala's lakes and oceans.
Caimans, iguanas, and other
reptiles live on the shore.

caiman

17

The People

Long ago, a people called the Maya lived in Guatemala. Spain conquered the Maya in the 1500s. Today, Spanish is the national language of Guatemala. It is spoken by most people. But many people still speak one of the Mayan languages.

Almost half the people in Guatemala are descended from the Maya.

Celebrations

Guatemalans celebrate many holidays. Many villages have a **patron saint**. People celebrate their saint's day. They dress in fancy clothes and eat special foods.

September 15 is <u>Independence Day</u> in Guatemala. It celebrates the day in 1821 when Guatemala won its freedom from Spain.

Words to Keep

capital: the city that is home to the government

coat of arms: the special sign of a nation in the shape of a shield

independent: free from the control of others

patron saint: a holy man or woman who protects a place

rain forest: a thick forest found in places that are hot and wet

wildlife preserves: places where animals and plants are safe from harm

Learn More at the Library

Books (Check out these books to learn more.)

Knudsen, Shannon. *Guatemala*. Lerner Publications, 2011.

Rudolph, Jessica. *Guatemala*. Bearport Publishing, 2016.

Schuetz, Kari. *Guatemala*. Bellwether Media, 2012.

Web Sites (Ask an adult to show you these web sites.)

Ducksters for Kids
http://www.ducksters.com/geography/country.php?country=Guatemala

Science Facts for Kids
http://easyscienceforkids.com/all-about-guatemala/

National Geographic for Kids
http://kids.nationalgeographic.com/explore/countries/guatemala/

Tikal is an old Maya city.

Index

About the Author

Joanne Mattern has written hundreds of nonfiction books for children. She likes writing about different people and places. Joanne lives in New York State with her family.